THIS JOURNAL BELONGS TO:

First published in Great Britain in 2018 by Orion Spring,
An imprint of the Orion Publishing group Ltd
Carmelite House
50 Victoria Embankment
London EC4Y 0DZ
An Hachette UK Company

1 3 5 7 9 10 8 6 4 2

A CIP catalogue record for this book is available from the British Library.

ISBN: 9781409183136

Design: Ben Gardiner
Production Controller: Katie Horrocks
Black and white illustrations: Fearne Cotton
All other colour illustrations: Jessica May Underwood
With thanks to Rebecca Dennis for the breathing exercises on 17 July and
15 August, originally printed in *Calm* by Fearne Cotton.

Printed in Italy

www.orionbooks.co.uk

ORION
SPRING

FEARNE COTTON

CALM

THE JOURNAL

WRITING OUT YOUR DAILY STRESSES TO HELP YOU
FIND YOUR PEACEFUL CENTRE

HELLO!

Welcome to Calm: *the journal*. A space waiting to be filled with your thoughts, concerns, feelings and a little fun too. The idea behind this bound chunk of peace is to focus us on welcoming the calm on board. It is a place for us to vent our stresses and expel our frustrations without judgement or pressure. It's a chance to put old-fashioned pen to paper to untangle what is floating around in our minds and create less tension around those things that cause constant rumination or concern.

I love talking to friends or people I trust when I feel spun out (which believe me is quite often) but I also cherish the process of writing down my thoughts to better understand them. It has proved very therapeutic for me over the years through writing my books and keeping personal journals at home. Sometimes we feel confused about ideas, relationships or matters of injustice, or frustrated because of time wasted or our own depleted energy levels. Our heads feel foggy and congested and in turn our bodies mimic their so-called leader: the mind. We mentally and physically feel stressed, sometimes even at breaking point. Our muscles may coil and tighten like rusty springs, headaches may spring up like pulsating bubbles of red-hot lava and words might get jumbled along the way. When we can't make sense of our own life's worries, how on earth can another? Writing down our thoughts and feelings freely without editing them allows us to gain a little clarity so we can then start to do some work or some letting go to help bring in the calm. Calm needs space to breathe. It needs grounded feet to establish itself and it needs deep rooted love to stick around. This book is all about remembering these points and bringing them into focus.

I get wound up about many of life's banal moments like I'm sure lots of you do too. At the other end of the spectrum, I also get physically het up when faced with the pure injustice, cruelty and suffering I see around me. I don't always know how to cope with these feelings in the moment. I feel caught up in the emotion and travel far from my place of calm. We all know that stress is not good for us. It's bad for our nervous system. It hinders sleep. It messes with our digestion. It pushes illness to the surface. It shatters relationships. It makes us lose sight of the good. No one is exempt from this and a lot of us could do with some help defusing it quicker. That's why I think a little self-inventory and a little time-out to write in a journal each day is particularly handy. Call it 'you-time' or simply see it as a moment of reflection: this book is an emotional mirror. Life is always going to throw us good and bad so we must look within to find our own coping mechanisms and our own sense of calm.

Once we have taken a look in the mirror and noticed our own part in it all we can then work out whether we are ready to try something new, whether that be practically or a thought process. There are always small steps we can take towards a calmer existence if we are willing to really look at ourselves.

I really hope you enjoy scribbling down whatever your mind throws up and find calm and relief in giving yourself the time and space to honour whatever those words turn out to be.

This book has got your back. It won't judge you or answer back. Open up to its blank embrace and feel the calm roll in as you let those words and their emotion loosen their grip.

Grab that pen, and welcome in some calm.

HOW TO USE
THIS BOOK

I'm not a fan of rules so don't wish to administer any to you whatso-
ever. There is no such thing as a 'wrong' way to use these pages, as it
is all about YOU! I have offered up moments and questions for each
day of the year that may prompt or spur on your own emotions and
understanding so you can perhaps dig a little deeper, or try something new if it feels right. But this part of the book is merely a little
'guide' if you will. If you want to ignore the prompts and write something totally different, go for it! You can scribble, draw, doodle, write
a poem, an answer, a question back at the question – it's a creative
free-for-all to help release tension and create calm.

You'll see that each month is themed with a subject that feels pertinent to the particular time of year. It will hopefully marry with your natural and seasonal thoughts and help take you down a path of inner discovery and freedom. When you're filling in the journal feel free to focus on this theme or keep it at the back of your mind if you have other pressing matters to concentrate on.

You'll also find a mini reflection spiral on each diary entry which looks like this: ⊚ . Mark on the spiral how calm you are feeling each day; the outer point being big stress and the inner circle being divine peace. This is helpful because at the end of the year you can flick through the book to see if your stress levels have changed for the better.

Remember, this is your space to do what you need to, so express it, my friend, and don't hold back! May the calm be with you!

JANUARY

Hello, New Year! A chance to start again, an opportunity to turn over a new leaf and break habits of old. It is also the month where we can feel burdened by expectation, the heat of the pressure to keep self-made promises and resolutions; and the heavy weight of an empty purse. It's a high-octane month where we are acutely aware of how everyone else is planning to conquer the world with new gym memberships and vats of green juice.

While some will glide in to the New Year in their shiny boots purchased in the January sales feeling nothing but glee, a lot of us will be trudging behind, reluctant to remove our Christmas sweaters, knowing we shouldn't really continue to eat mince pies and colourfully wrapped choccies before 9am each day. We sit staring at 12 blank months in front of us wondering how we might get off to the best start to propel us in the right direction for optimum achievement and a better version of ourselves. PRESSURE! Oh, and it's bloody freezing. So how do we step into January feeling calm, unnerved by the noise of other people's goals and sky-high aims, and remain balanced when spring seems so far away?

This month is about being kind to ourselves. Self-care – a phrase that can curl toes and shudder cheeks. In the UK we are not so good at this one but hey, there's a first time for everything. Can you make your New Year's goal one of self-love, care and understanding? Rather than dashing into January with a pile of rules and restriction, let's make it a month for simply focusing on the little changes that make a huge difference to our own state of mind. Small pleasures, tiny moments of appreciation for simply being you, and tip-toed footsteps in the right direction. Whether it's with a green juice in hand or a frothy hot chocolate, be kind to yourself and let the calm flood in.

1 JANUARY

Start the year with a list
of what you hope the next
12 months will bring: all
you want to see, hear,
experience and feel.
Alongside these dreams
and aspirations, bear in
mind some self-care when
you put pen to paper.
It's brilliant to have goals
set but don't pile on the
pressure and do leave time
to relax and take stock.

. . . .

. . . .

. . . .

. . . .

. . . .

. . . .

. . . .

. . . .

. . . .

. . . .

. . . .

. . . .

. . . .

. . . .

. . . .

. . . .

. . . .

2 JANUARY

Now all the Christmas decorations are packed away (well they are in my house anyway) and the family gatherings have perhaps petered out, remember how good it felt to connect with others. Why not have a group of your favourite people over for a spot of dinner or even just a cuppa? Put your phones away and just sit and enjoy each other's company.

. . . .
. . . .
. . . .
. . . .
. . . .
. . . .
. . . .
. . . .
. . . .
. . . .
. . . .
. . . .
. . . .
. . . .
. . . .
. . . .

3 JANUARY

The excess of Christmas makes most of us feel pretty groggy. Care for your gut and you'll feel much happier and calmer all round. For the next five days, keep a log of what you eat and how you feel half-an-hour after each meal. Note which foods make you feel balanced and which foods leave you bloated and uncomfortable, and perhaps leave them off the menu next time.

I ATE . . .	30 MINS LATER I FELT . . .
BREAKFAST:	
LUNCH:	
DINNER:	
SNACKS/DRINKS:	
CONCLUSIONS:	

4 JANUARY

Day 2 of your calm-gut food log. What worked for you and didn't work for you today?

I ATE . . .	30 MINS LATER I FELT . . .
BREAKFAST:	
LUNCH:	
DINNER:	
SNACKS/DRINKS:	
CONCLUSIONS:	

" WHENEVER YOU FIND YOURSELF DOUBTING HOW FAR YOU CAN GO, JUST REMEMBER HOW FAR YOU HAVE COME. "

5 JANUARY

Keep your food log going, noticing how your gut feels throughout the day. Notice anything different today?

I ATE . . .	30 MINS LATER I FELT . . .
BREAKFAST:	
LUNCH:	
DINNER:	
SNACKS/DRINKS:	
CONCLUSIONS:	

6 JANUARY

Day 4 of your calm-gut food log. How do you feel today? Which foods are making your energy levels soar – without causing an energy crash afterwards?

I ATE . . .	30 MINS LATER I FELT . . .
BREAKFAST:	
LUNCH:	
DINNER:	
SNACKS/DRINKS:	
CONCLUSIONS:	

7 JANUARY

Are there any ingredients that are causing you discomfort? Are you still eating too much sugar from Christmas time? Is it causing your gut to cry out for help?

I ATE . . .	30 MINS LATER I FELT . . .
BREAKFAST:	
LUNCH:	
DINNER:	
SNACKS/DRINKS:	
CONCLUSIONS:	

8 JANUARY

Look back on your five-day food diary. Are there any changes you can make to your diet now you know a bit more about works for you?

. . . .

. . . .

. . . .

. . . .

. . . .

. . . .

. . . .

. . . .

9 JANUARY

Do you notice any patterns of eating when you feel stressed vs happy? Do you reach for sugar for comfort and – if you do – does it make you feel lousy afterwards? If you're craving sugar reach for some good fats like nuts and seeds. If you're low on energy go for fruit over chocolate.

10 JANUARY

The New Year is a great time to switch things up a little. Perhaps try going vegetarian or even vegan for one day a week and see if the waterfall of vitamin C makes a difference to how you feel. There are so many recipes to choose from online.

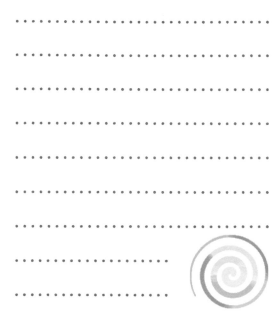

. . . .

. . . .

. . . .

. . . .

. . . .

. . . .

. . . .

. . . .

. . . .

11 JANUARY

Does this year feel like an exciting blank canvas or a little scary and unknown?

. . . .

. . . .

. . . .

. . . .

. . . .

. . . .

. . . .

. . . .

. . . .

12 JANUARY

Whether you over did it at Christmas or had too many people to buy presents for, many of us can feel stressed about money at this time of year. Can you save some cash this month by cutting out the booze, dry January style? Instead of a night in the pub or a bottle of wine with mates can you instead have a small gathering where each friend brings a dish? Yummy food and at a shared cost?

. . . .

. . . .

. . . .

. . . .

. . . .

. . . .

. . . .

. . . .

13 JANUARY

What does self-care mean to you?

. . . .

. . . .

. . . .

. . . .

. . . .

. . . .

. . . .

. . . .

14 JANUARY

How do you feel today?
Have you been caring
for yourself a little more
this year? Look back to
yesterday's entry and
apply everything you
already know.

. . . .
. . . .
. . . .
. . . .
. . . .
. . . .
. . . .
. . . .

15 JANUARY

It is cold and the sun still
sets rather early during this
never-ending month, so why
not make the most of the
long winter nights. Never
underestimate the cosiness
and tranquillity of simply
lighting some candles, either
while you eat your dinner or
as you snuggle under a blanket
with a book.

. . . .
. . . .
. . . .
. . . .
. . . .
. . . .
. . . .
. . . .

16 JANUARY

If you have young children, work nights or suffer with insomnia you'll more than likely think of sleep as somewhat of a luxury. Getting the right amount of quality sleep is essential to our wellbeing and health. Log here how many hours of sleep you got last night.

....

....

....

....

....

....

....

....

....

17 JANUARY

If you find yourself doing too much before bedtime, perhaps try winding down and getting into bed earlier tonight. You'll feel brighter and fresher tomorrow morning and ready for a brand new day.

....

....

....

....

....

....

....

....

....

18 JANUARY

Did you sleep well last
night? Did you have any
dreams you remember?

. . . .

. . . .

. . . .

. . . .

. . . .

. . . .

. . . .

. . . .

. . . .

19 JANUARY

Write down a list of ways
you know you could be
kinder to yourself.

. . . .

. . . .

. . . .

. . . .

. . . .

. . . .

. . . .

. . . .

. . . .

20 JANUARY

We all beat ourselves up
at times and can be very
self-critical. What parts of
your life do you think you
over-analyse and criticise?

....

....

....

....

....

....

....

....

....

....

....

....

....

....

....

....

....

....

....

....

21 JANUARY

Could you be kinder
to your body? Do you
criticise your own body
and obsess over parts of it?
Can you show those body
parts a bit more love?

....
....
....
....
....
....
....
....

22 JANUARY

How much time do you
spend on your phone? Can
you decrease this duration
and spend more time day-
dreaming, brainstorming or
simply observing? It's all
about slowing down our
thoughts.

....
....
....
....
....
....
....

23 JANUARY

Do you constantly put others first? Do you think you must please all of those around you? Can you think of an example where you could have, and probably should have, put yourself first?

24 JANUARY

Write a list of all of the activities you know calm you down. Whether it's a hobby or part of your daily routine, remember it, write it down and honour it.

25 JANUARY

Do you spend enough time on your own? If not, maybe it's time to see how it feels. Take yourself off for a solo walk at lunchtime or turn your phone off so you're unconnected from others and more connected to yourself. How does it feel? Did you notice anything different in your patter of thoughts or behaviour?

26 JANUARY

Can you write down the
last time you were kind to
yourself and how it felt?

....

....

....

....

....

....

....

....

....

27 JANUARY

Write down the last
time you were hard on
yourself. Looking back
could things have been
different? Can you
forgive yourself for not
being your best in that
moment?

....

....

....

....

....

....

....

....

28 JANUARY

Accept that some days our best will be sky-high and other days our best will be mediocre. When we remember our limits are malleable and ever-changing, we can learn to give ourselves a break when things don't go as planned.

"DEAR FUTURE, I'M READY."

29 JANUARY

If you're working towards a big goal for the year ahead or simply trying to limit the fear around something pending, remember small steps in the right direction are just as important, if not more so, than giant leaps.

30 JANUARY

Have a lovely hot bath or a steamy shower and enjoy the sensation of the water on your skin. Remember, being in the moment involves taking notice of all of our senses. Having a bath is a great tangible way to reduce stress and get in the NOW.

31 JANUARY

We made it through the
'Monday' of months!
Hooray! What moments
or people brought you
calm this month?

....
....
....
....
....
....
....
....
....
....
....
....
....
....
....
....
....
....
....

FEBRUARY

Acceptance is one of the hardest concepts to truly live by but also one of the most freeing. February is a great month to practise this one as I always find at this point my threshold and tolerance for the winter is at breaking point. My energy levels aren't always great; my skin feels dry; and I have never-ending colds that my children kindly bring home from school. To say I'm 'over it' is an understatement. This is when I go on Instagram and see that others may be on an exotic retreat, tanned legs stretched out with book in lap and fluorescent cocktail nearby. I make assumptions about others, feel the green-eyed monster rear its jealous head and compare myself to others. All utterly pointless.

Accepting the seasons and all that come with them is a good way of noticing our own tolerance for circumstances occurring in our lives. I always feel a jolt of surprise when I see the first daffodil pop through the damp soil mid-Feb. A small reminder that spring WILL happen. We just have to let go and let nature do its thing – much like in life. There are many things we cannot change or speed up or wish away, and accept-ance really is the key to unlocking ourselves from habitual stagnancy and draining repetition of behaviour, and instead stepping towards a calmer existence. If you're ready to give it a go, I am!

1 FEBRUARY

How do you feel about this time of year? Do you take advantage of the dark evenings and snuggle down or do you lust after warmer times and flip-flops? How does February make you feel?

. . . .

. . . .

. . . .

. . . .

. . . .

. . . .

. . . .

. . . .

. . . .

2 FEBRUARY

Are you constantly trying to change yourself? What personal attributes do you think you should be more accepting of?

. . . .

. . . .

. . . .

. . . .

. . . .

. . . .

. . . .

. . . .

. . . .

3 FEBRUARY

Are there bad habits you know you need to get rid of this year? Make a list of them here.

....

....

....

....

....

....

....

....

4 FEBRUARY

Which people in life do you find hard to deal with? Are there any tricky characters that push your buttons? Can you make any changes your end or if not, at least try and accept that you'll maybe never get along?

....

....

....

....

....

....

....

....

5 FEBRUARY

How good are you at accepting the behaviour of those around you when it differs greatly to yours? This could be an individual or group of people. As well as noticing the differences that are present, can you see any connections you have with them? Having similarities with people who grate on us can be irritating, but can also lead us to empathise with that person.

6 FEBRUARY

Are there uncomfortable moments from the past that you replay over and over in your head? How can you help yourself accept those moments? This one can be very tricky especially if the memory was a traumatic experience. Is there a small chunk of the story you can accept so you can start to let it go?

Acceptance isn't about running from or ignoring injustice and pain. It's about helping us reach a calmer place so we can then act on the aforementioned in a helpful way. Shouting and ranting about injustice does very little. Proactively helping others or making changes allows us to take responsibility and react in a calmer manner.

8 FEBRUARY

Is there anything that's frustrating you in life currently? Sometimes just admitting it to yourself and putting pen to paper is the first step to making positive and calming changes.

. . . .

. . . .

. . . .

. . . .

. . . .

. . . .

. . . .

. . . .

. . . .

9 FEBRUARY

In this day and age where we can voyeuristically spy on others through social media and thereby compare ourselves to so many, it can be hard to remember our own strengths in the fog of others' stories. Can you spot them and celebrate them?

. . . .

. . . .

. . . .

. . . .

. . . .

. . . .

. . . .

. . . .

10 FEBRUARY

Can you, with open arms, accept all the beauty around you? Do you find it hard to be greeted with good times and happiness? Do you ever push it away?

....

....

....

....

....

....

....

....

11 FEBRUARY

It can feel utterly cringe to admit we like parts of ourselves – whether that be physically or our personality. But you know what? We should take time to accept and celebrate all of our good bits. Here's your chance. No one's watching, no one will judge. Go for it!

....

....

....

....

....

....

....

....

12 FEBRUARY

Do you ever get stuck in the habit of only talking about the negative, perhaps gossiping or picking fault with others? Can you accept that this might not be the best route to calm? Can you take a step back from this habitual behaviour and speak more positively?

....
....
....
....
....
....
....
....
....

13 FEBRUARY

Do you look for chaos in life or do you welcome the calm wholeheartedly? Do you enjoy those calm moments as much as the exciting times?

....
....
....
....
....
....
....
....
....

14 FEBRUARY

The day of love. Do you feel loved? Are you loving enough? Are you accepting of your current situation? Happily single? Content in union? Or unsure of where you feel calmest and happiest?

15 FEBRUARY

Are you accepting of imperfection? How does imperfection make you feel?

"YOU TOTALLY CAN."

16 FEBRUARY

Remember the
importance of making
mistakes. Remember
how it can lead you down
interesting paths, teach
you so much and open up
your empathy to others.

. . . .

. . . .

. . . .

. . . .

. . . .

. . . .

. . . .

. . . .

. . . .

17 FEBRUARY

Do you think those
around you are accepting
of you and your life
choices? If not, how does
that make you feel?

. . . .

. . . .

. . . .

. . . .

. . . .

. . . .

. . . .

. . . .

. . . .

18 FEBRUARY

Are you accepting of silence? If not, can you learn to enjoy it? With so much noise ricocheting around today's culture it can feel almost wrong to sit in silence. Give it a go for a few minutes now.

. . . .
. . . .
. . . .
. . . .
. . . .
. . . .
. . . .
. . . .
. . . .

19 FEBRUARY

Have you noticed any flowers blooming yet?

. . . .
. . . .
. . . .
. . . .
. . . .
. . . .
. . . .
. . . .
. . . .

20 FEBRUARY

Have you had any particularly 'calm' moments this month? If so, what were they?

....

....

....

....

....

....

....

....

....

21 FEBRUARY

Accepting who you are, what you look like, how you deal with life and all those you may have attracted to you allows us to celebrate our own unique magic. What do you think yours is?

....

....

....

....

....

....

....

....

22 FEBRUARY

Accepting compliments
can feel very unnatural
and un-British at times.
What is your reaction
when presented with a
kind remark?

. . . .
. . . .
. . . .
. . . .
. . . .
. . . .
. . . .
. . . .
. . . .

23 FEBRUARY

Accepting other people's
bad behaviour that has
personally affected you can
be very tricky. Can you
accept a past mistake from
another and silently forgive
them? Free yourself
from the shackles of their
behaviour and watch the
tension float away.

. . . .
. . . .
. . . .
. . . .
. . . .
. . . .
. . . .
. . . .
. . . .

24 FEBRUARY

Draw of picture of what you think you and your body look like.

25 FEBRUARY

Do you ever get struck with a fatal blow of FOMO? I mean, who doesn't? Can you accept that you might be home alone on a cold February evening while others are out having fun? Maybe, just maybe, you're feeling a lot happier and calmer than they are anyway!

26 FEBRUARY

How do you take loss in life? Loss of a job, a friend, a loved one or a community, can feel very traumatic and stressful. Previously how have you dealt with loss?

....
....
....
....
....
....
....
....
....

27 FEBRUARY

Have you ever experienced loss but also gained from the same situation? Perhaps it was clarity, a friend, a new experience or appreciation of life?

....
....
....
....
....
....
....
....

28/29   **FEBRUARY**

What moments or people brought you calm this month?

. . . .

. . . .

. . . .

. . . .

. . . .

. . . .

. . . .

. . . .

. . . .

. . . .

. . . .

. . . .

. . . .

. . . .

. . . .

MARCH

Are you one of those people who springs out of bed in the morning, buzzing with ideas for the day ahead, or does it take you a while to get your head in gear with the idea that you have a whole new day to get through? Or maybe you oscillate between the two?

Let's make March about motivation. Some may associate 'calm' with being still, doing less than usual or perhaps even being static. I believe it is the exact opposite. I personally feel the most calm when I'm in the midst of a brainwave about a new work project or idea, or when out running in the park. When I feel sloth-like and stagnant I actually feel much more chaotic internally. My head whirrs with conflict about which direction I should move in and my body feels stiff yet agitated. Movement and flow is the key to calm. Keeping our bodies flowing, but also our feelings, thoughts and emotions. That doesn't mean we get to skip feeling sad, angry, let down or any other negative emotion that might come our way, but it does mean we can let that feeling come in and then leave again naturally. Holding on to emotion and stress is very unhealthy for us all and the longer we hold on to it the harder it is to let it flow out again.

Spring is also on the way this month so there is change all around us. Bulbs poking their heads out from beneath our feet, leaves fleshing out our favourite trees and skies perhaps brightening in their sapphire tones to lift our spirits. Look for the flow this month wherever you go. Seek it out in nature, notice your own emotional patterns and get your body moving and awakening like the daffodils and tulips that are springing into action.

1 MARCH

Are you feeling motivated at the start of this new month? What do you feel motivated about?

. . . .
. . . .
. . . .
. . . .
. . . .
. . . .
. . . .
. . . .

2 MARCH

What do you need a little help with in life? Do you feel a little stuck in any area? Do you struggle with physically motivating yourself or are you resisting sorting out a more emotional situation in your life?

. . . .
. . . .
. . . .
. . . .
. . . .
. . . .
. . . .
. . . .

3 MARCH

Can you take a walk today? Whether it's walking to university or work, or out strolling with your baby in the buggy. Get your comfiest trainers on, stick some headphones in with your favourite music or podcast (if you're on your own) and get moving! Even if it's just for half an hour, it'll leave you feeling motivated for the rest of the day.

4 MARCH

Do you have an exercise plan? By this I don't mean a personal trainer or strict schedule; I mean do you feel motivated to regularly go and get your blood pumping? If no, what exercise do you think you'd enjoy? Finding a sport, class or activity you enjoy makes exercise so much easier.

5 MARCH

Is there a pipe dream or idea you would love to have a go at but have never felt like it was the right time? Could the right time be NOW?

. . . .
. . . .
. . . .
. . . .
. . . .
. . . .
. . . .
. . . .
. . . .

6 MARCH

Is stagnancy residing in any parts of your life? Do you feel stuck at all?

. . . .
. . . .
. . . .
. . . .
. . . .
. . . .
. . . .
. . . .

Do you need some motivation
to make a decision right now?
Are you in mental conflict
about which road to choose?
Stop the procrastinating, step
out of limbo-land and make a
decision today.

8   MARCH

Do you like to step
outside your comfort
zone? When was the last
time you did it?

·································

·································

·································

·································

·································

·································

·································

·································

·································

9   MARCH

Dare to do something
different today! Whether
it's a new route to work,
an activity after work
one evening or eating
something you don't
normally.

·································

·································

·································

·································

·································

·································

·································

·································

·································

10 MARCH

What bad habits do you have?
Do you often eat something
that you know doesn't agree
with you? Do you react in
the same way every time a
certain someone annoys you?
Do you often think badly of
yourself? Can you endeavour
to try to make a small change
to those habits this month?
Small changes can lead to big
moments of calm and clarity.

11 MARCH

When was the last time
you felt truly motivated
and saw results? How did
that feel?

"IF YOU KNOW YOU CAN DO BETTER . . . THEN DO BETTER."

12 MARCH

This month is the proud owner of Mother's Day. Whether you have a mum, step mum or memories of a late mum, make sure you have a calm moment of thanks when thinking about them. Even if that relationship is or was tricky, focusing on gratitude and the positives allows us to feel rooted in calm and yet energised at the same time.

13 MARCH

How do we get back to feeling motivated when we have failed or feel like we should just give up? Often finding new routes as a result can prove to be a wonderful silver lining in the face of upset and disappointment.

14 MARCH

If you have a mum and want to show her thanks, why not gift her some calm? Take her for a peaceful spring-time walk or a tranquil coffee and natter. What would your mum class as calm and can you make that happen for her?

. . . .

. . . .

. . . .

. . . .

. . . .

. . . .

. . . .

. . . .

. . . .

15 MARCH

Who around you inspires you?

. . . .

. . . .

. . . .

. . . .

. . . .

. . . .

. . . .

. . . .

. . . .

16 MARCH

If someone unhelpful
tells you, 'you can't do it',
'you're not good enough',
'that's not quite right', or
'you will definitely fail' . . .
DO IT ANYWAY.

17 MARCH

Do you feel motivated
to help another person?
Sometimes when our own
problems or stress in life
feel extreme, it is a relief to
help someone else. Do you
know someone who needs
a friendly pick-me-up, a
helping hand or words of
advice. Can you be that
shoulder to lean on?

18   MARCH

I love having a good old
spring clean and culling
loads of unnecessaries in
my house. Do you need
to do the same? Do you
feel you would benefit
from less clutter and more
space? If you live with
other people, could you
motivate them to help you
in your cleaning mission?

19   MARCH

Play some music that
motivates you today!
Music can be so very
encouraging.

20 MARCH

Draw a picture or brainstorm what motivation looks like to you.

21 MARCH

Write a list of things you'd like to achieve this year. They don't have to be huge goals, just little snippets of joy, contentment or ideas you would like to come to fruition.

. . . .

. . . .

. . . .

. . . .

. . . .

. . . .

. . . .

. . . .

. . . .

22 MARCH

Towards the end of March each year, the clocks ping forward bringing us more daylight in the evenings and hopefully a little spring in our step along the way. How will you use that extra hour of daylight?

. . . .

. . . .

. . . .

. . . .

. . . .

. . . .

. . . .

. . . .

23 MARCH

It is more than likely chilly out, which is enough to make you want to fashion a coat out of a duvet and stay inside all day. I know that if I'm feeling a little tense or lacklustre, a good walk come rain or shine gives me a huge boost physically and mentally.

24 MARCH

Is there something you've been putting off for some time? Boring paperwork? Confrontation? An important email? Some studying? Make TODAY the day! You can do it!

25 MARCH

Nature is all around us if we open our eyes to it. It can be the most inspiring observation if we truly stop and watch. Take a moment today away from your smartphone to look around and soak up the natural surroundings. Even if you are living or working in a large town or city, watch a bird swoop and glide through the sky. Watch the leaves flutter on a nearby tree. Let the simple rule over the complicated and sometimes unnecessary in life. Be inspired by nature.

26 MARCH

What colour inspires you? What colours make you feel vibrant and alive? Can you wear a colour today that complements your desire for action and life?

27 MARCH

Do you ever feel envious or even jealous of someone in your life? Can you switch up that energy and turn that envy into a catalyst for change? Can you feel inspired instead? What is it about this particular person or group of people that you envy? Do you really want what they have or are you focusing on what you lack?

28 MARCH

Not that I'm one for wishing away time but, my God, there is a palpable sigh of relief as March ends and April begins. Of course April can still be laden with dripping umbrellas and unflattering anoraks, but it can also be home to the odd picnic and open-toed shoe. What are you looking forward to this spring?

29 MARCH

Do you ever get into the habit of saying 'no'? Whether it be out of fear or simply habitual, it can be invigorating to say a big fat 'YES' every now and then. 'Do you want to join me this Wednesday for a local reggae/salsa/line dancing night?'. . . Me: 'Ah nooyessssss please, I would love to.' Why the hell not?

30 MARCH

Don't forget to laugh! I often get so wrapped up in the logistics of life as a working mum that I forget how good it feels to laugh. Instant happiness and instant calm! Look through old photos; call up your mates; reminisce; or watch a funny film. Laughter is such a tonic.

31 MARCH

What moments or people brought you calm this month?

....

....

....

....

....

....

....

....

....

....

....

....

....

....

....

APRIL

Ahhh April, you big breezy breath of fresh air – I LOVE YOU! With your optimism and rosy pink blossom. I often feel like I'm shedding a skin this month. We are all quite literally peeling off the layers as the puffa jackets get stored away and the odd light raincoat may be tentatively worn instead. But I also feel like physically and mentally I'm letting go of the winter and welcoming with pasty arms the spring and the NEW!

How do you deal with change? Whenever we experience the transition of a season we are reminded about the importance of change, and with it, excitement – or sometimes fear. The seasons and indeed nature are there as an obvious and constant reminder of how we must learn to flow through change and not get too stuck. Feeling stuck or trapped or too scared to move forward is never a calm place to be. Free flowing and malleable is what we are all probably aiming for but sometimes it can be easier said than done. Make this the month to notice, accept and welcome change into your life.

1 APRIL

I bloody hate practical
jokes, but hey, if you
must!

....

....

....

....

....

....

....

....

2 APRIL

Are you ready to let go
of the last few months
and truly welcome in the
new? Do you feel there
are certain experiences or
memories that you need
to shake off?

....

....

....

....

....

....

....

....

3   APRIL

How do you physically feel
as you enter a brand new
month and season?

. . . .

. . . .

. . . .

. . . .

. . . .

. . . .

. . . .

. . . .

. . . .

4   APRIL

How do you face change?
Are there many changes
afoot in your life at the
moment?

. . . .

. . . .

. . . .

. . . .

. . . .

. . . .

. . . .

. . . .

. . . .

"BE AFRAID
AND DO IT
ANYWAY. "

5 APRIL

Change doesn't have to mean switching things up with such haste that you don't follow commitments or ideas through. Perseverance isn't to be underestimated. If you have goals that are taking time to complete or get off the ground then use this month to work out other calm ways to attract movement in the right direction.

6 APRIL

Sometimes we spot signs in life that show us change is needed. These signs may have been around for a while, we just haven't quite got the message or acted on them before. Can you make this the month you act on them?

If you recognise signs in your life that you think mean change is needed, what might you be able to do about it? Are there tiny steps that could be taken on tiptoes in the right direction? Remember change can be teeny tiny and still have huge impact and force in the long run.

8   APRIL

I'm not sure there's a
human on earth who
doesn't want to change
at least one thing about
themselves. Me? . . .
the list is long! Some I
can realistically sort, but
some are just the essence
of who I am and I have
to learn to honour that.
Possibly even celebrate
them. Can you try too?

9   APRIL

Have you noticed any
differences in your
behaviour or thought
patterns since writing in
this journal? Does it feel
helpful to take a self-
inventory each day?

10 APRIL

What changes can you see around you in nature? Have the trees started to blossom? Are the birds singing a little louder?

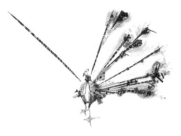

. . . .

. . . .

. . . .

. . . .

. . . .

. . . .

. . . .

. . . .

11 APRIL

Are there any changes around you that are troubling you? Perhaps short-term worries relating to family and friends or linked to how society is changing constantly around us? Writing them down may help make sense of them a little or take a bit of the weight off your shoulders.

. . . .

. . . .

. . . .

. . . .

. . . .

. . . .

. . . .

. . . .

12 APRIL

Looking back over your
life, what changes have
been profoundly positive?

....
....
....
....
....
....
....
....

13 APRIL

Do you have any regrets?
I can't honestly say I have
none. Maybe one day I will be
at peace with some of them,
but currently I still have a list
as long as my arm. And that's
okay!

....
....
....
....
....
....
....
....

14 APRIL

Are you having trouble making a decision? Are you at a crossroads and feeling far from calm? Can you use this space to write a pros and cons list to weigh up the outcomes?

15 APRIL

What changes did you think would or should have happened for you already in your life that have NOT? Can you work out why? Is it because fear surrounds making moves in a certain direction or do you feel bad luck is whipping the carpet from under your feet?

16 APRIL

Do you ever feel eager to change things in your life because you feel uncomfortable? A strange edgy feeling that makes you reach for newness rather than sitting with the feeling? Can you trace back to where this feeling comes from?

17 APRIL

Sitting with an uncomfortable feeling can often be as important as trying to change it. For example, I sometimes feel edgy and can't work out why, so reach for a snack or my phone to escape the discomfort of the moment. Sitting with the feeling is much more useful to try to get to the bottom of what is actually irking me.

18 APRIL

Do you truly accept yourself? At times I really don't. I want to be better, smarter, quicker, fitter, kinder, without realising that with this list in place I'm leaving no room to just be ME. Can you write here why you are brilliant as you are without making any changes to yourself? No matter what your demons tell you, you are brilliant as you are.

19 APRIL

Has your day been a calm one? What would you have changed?

. . . .

. . . .

. . . .

. . . .

. . . .

. . . .

. . . .

. . . .

20 APRIL

Making a change can be nerve-wracking but not impossible. Make a list here of all the scary 'first's you've conquered to remind yourself that you are more than capable.

. . . .

. . . .

. . . .

. . . .

. . . .

. . . .

. . . .

. . . .

21 APRIL

Why not try a new meal today?
Cook something you would
never normally try. Seek
out the random spice you've
never heard of at your local
supermarket; use the grill pan
you've not even got out of the
box; or peer into the dusty
pages of that cookbook you've
got stuffed at the back of your
cupboard behind the tea towels.

22 APRIL

Is there anything you notice about yourself that changes at this time of year? Are you more optimistic? More adventurous? More empowered by change?

23 APRIL

How have you changed over the years? Are you a little more confident? Perhaps a teeny bit wrinklier or softer? A tad more tolerant? What changes are you proud of?

24 APRIL

How have the important relationships in your life changed over time? Do you put more or less time into these connections? Is more face-to-face time required? The odd handwritten note? Text someone now to arrange a cup of tea and good old-fashioned catch-up.

25 APRIL

Why not change up a room in your house? My husband will regularly find me lugging a coffee table across a room in an effort to spruce up the energy and alter the feeling of a room. It gives such a freshness and new perspective on the space around us.

26 APRIL

On the next sunny day this month make sure to pop your face outside and soak up the vitamin D. It can feel like we have been in hibernation for months on end at the beginning of spring and we forget how good it feels to have sunshine on our skin. Just don't forget your SPF, even if it's still a little cool.

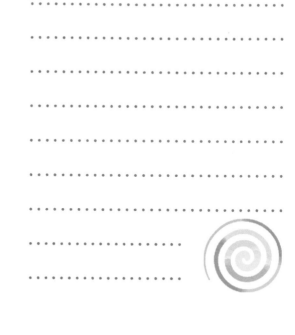

27 APRIL

Are you in the middle of a big change? Have you experienced one in the past? What are your go-to emotions when in the midst of change? Are you spun out in a whirl of stress and chaos or are you awoken to possibility and adventure?

" **DON'T LOOK BACK, YOU'RE NOT GOING THAT WAY.** "

28 APRIL

Has your family set-up ever changed? It is more than likely that you will have experienced marriage, death, the birth of angel babes, divorce, or emigration at some point in your lifetime. How have you dealt with this movement? Are you still working it out now?

. . . .

. . . .

. . . .

. . . .

. . . .

. . . .

. . . .

. . . .

. . . .

29 APRIL

Close your eyes (after you've read this entry obvs) and then visualise the change you so desire. Is it a personal habit? A location or job? Can you strongly visualise not only the change but the result? Picture it vividly like you're watching a film at the cinema.

. . . .

. . . .

. . . .

. . . .

. . . .

. . . .

. . . .

. . . .

. . . .

30 APRIL

What moments or people brought you calm this month?

. . . .

. . . .

. . . .

. . . .

. . . .

. . . .

. . . .

. . . .

. . . .

. . . .

. . . .

. . . .

. . . .

. . . .

. . . .

MAY

Now we are into the swing of things and are hopefully feeling the calm benefits of writing our thoughts down (teamed with the odd sunny day in the park!), let's delve a little deeper. Let's take a look outside ourselves, step out of our over-thinking, worrying brains and properly see and feel what is going on around us.

Let's open that drawer in the kitchen which has become a home to all obsolete and miscellaneous items. Let's peel back curtains and view what is happening outside on the pavement. Let's see how our mess or order, and general collection of objects, mirrors how we feel and are living.

This month it's time to open up to how much our surroundings affect us, whether that be at home, work or where we choose to spend our time. From properly taking an inventory of what is around us, we can learn a lot about ourselves, and how we change it can impact our lives and levels of calm for the better. Grab ya duster, let's go!

1   MAY

Perfect day for a
spring-clean, no?

. . . .
. . . .
. . . .
. . . .
. . . .
. . . .
. . . .
. . . .
. . . .
. . . .
. . . .
. . . .
. . . .
. . . .
. . . .
. . . .
. . . .
. . . .
. . . .
. . . .

2 MAY

Are there objects that you are
holding on to for the wrong
reasons? Sentimental but
perhaps in a slightly self-
torturing manner? Clearing
space and letting go of the
old is a great way of mentally
feeling a lot more clarity too. It
can be very hard, so make sure
you're getting rid of things
that you know are either not
needed or serve absolutely no
positive purpose.

3   MAY

Could you hold your own yard sale? Wait, we are not living in the sunny California hills or on the set of a teen soap! I mean, 'jumble sale'? Getting some mates or neighbours together, who could possibly bring their old bits and bobs too, can be such a fun way of letting go of the old and earning a bit of cash for you or a chosen charity.

. . . .

. . . .

. . . .

. . . .

. . . .

. . . .

. . . .

. . . .

. . . .

4   MAY

When you look around at the room you're in right now, how does it make you feel?

. . . .

. . . .

. . . .

. . . .

. . . .

. . . .

. . . .

. . . .

5 MAY

How do the colours make you
feel within your own home?
Do they make you feel calm?
Have you inherited wallpaper
that makes you feel slightly on
edge? Is there an opportunity
for change and freshness?
My husband has to almost
hide the light pink paint pots
in our house to stop me from
up-cycling furniture in this
calming and dreamy colour.

6 MAY

Do you hate opening
post and have a pile-up of
paperwork mounting up to
rival Everest? Face the fear
and get it opened and filed.
You'll feel such relief when
it's done.

7 MAY

Where is your calm spot?
A beach you have visited?
A friend's cosy home?
A clearing in a woodland
near your house? Why
does it feel so special?

. . . .
. . . .
. . . .
. . . .
. . . .
. . . .
. . . .
. . . .
. . . .

8 MAY

Which location make you
feel edgy? For me, I've
never been great in busy
and bustling cities. I feel
overwhelmed and slightly
chaotic. I obviously can't
avoid them the world over
forever but I do try to
actively seek out nature
and calm whenever I can.

. . . .
. . . .
. . . .
. . . .
. . . .
. . . .
. . . .
. . . .

9 MAY

What do you think your surroundings say about you? I'm a bit of a neat freak and I know deep down this is because I often feel out of control so this enforced order helps my mind to feel calmer and clearer.

10 MAY

Do you have many happy photos in your house? We have created a picture wall in our house where there are lots of tiny photos in frames with people we love staring back at us.

11 MAY

Can you recall a happy and calm memory in a particularly meaningful spot?

. . . .

. . . .

. . . .

. . . .

. . . .

. . . .

. . . .

. . . .

. . . .

12 MAY

Do you have many plants at home? I'm no Charlie Dimmock but this year I have cleared a space in our kitchen for small cacti and easy-to-care-for plants. They bring such life to the space and help to oxygenate the air.

. . . .

. . . .

. . . .

. . . .

. . . .

. . . .

. . . .

. . . .

. . . .

13 MAY

Do you often lose objects or necessary things in your home? Is there room for a little more organisation? My kids have so many Lego blocks and plastic creatures that usually make annoying noises or sing, so I find getting old gift boxes or wicker cases to store them in helps me feel less like my house is being overtaken by colourful, plastic chaos. It's much easier to locate things mid-tantrum too!

14 MAY

What is in your drawer of doom? Come on, we all have one! Ours is full of batteries, screwdrivers, cat collars, loyalty cards for coffee shops that no longer exist and Allen keys! Why do I have SO many Allen keys?! Shall we crack on and tackle that drawer then?

15 MAY

How do you wind down at night? I have to be extra vigilant with this one as I don't sleep too well. I know that I must have low lighting, no screens on, my phone on aeroplane mode and quiet in the run-up to bed. It's all part of my personal wind-down. Is this something that might help you to feel calmer before bed? What else might?

16 MAY

As the sun throws us a little more warmth and the wind blows a little less aggressively, don't forget to throw open those windows to let in some good old-fashioned fresh air.

17 MAY

Be careful who you let into your home. I think everyone that steps in to my home is leaving a little of their own story and energy here. Make sure the people you love come over often and the people you know hold a different kind of energy stay away if possible.

18 MAY

Are you getting outside enough? For those of us that are office-bound, work regularly indoors or run a home it can be the last thing on our minds, but is so, so important for our general wellbeing. Is there the opportunity to walk to work in the mornings, or can you ask a mate to join you for a walk in your lunchbreak?

19 MAY

Do you care about the
story of where your
possessions come from?
I love to buy vintage
clothing that has a
story and I also like
that it is helpful to the
environment. Upcycling
or buying second-hand
clothes or furniture can
be a lot of fun and a lot
cheaper too.

· ·

· ·

· ·

· ·

· ·

· ·

· ·

· · · · · · · · · · · · · · · · · · ·

· ·

20 MAY

If you have trouble letting
go of tangible objects
in your home and life,
can you trace back to
why? Does it mirror how
you perhaps hold on to
situations in life too?

· ·

· ·

· ·

· ·

· ·

· ·

· ·

· · · · · · · · · · · · · · · · · · ·

· ·

21 MAY

Do you have tough memories that are synonymous with a certain place? I do and it can be quite debilitating to have to go back to them. If you find yourself having to face a location that evokes fear or sorrow, picture a bubble of white light around you to help yourself visualise safety.

22 MAY

Where is your calm spot within your home? In the bath? On your favourite armchair?

23 MAY

Visualise letting go of an object or feeling that you know no longer serves you in your life. Close your eyes and imagine the object moving further and further towards the horizon until it becomes a tiny dot in the distance. Each time it moves a little further away, imagine that you physically and mentally feel lighter.

. . . .
. . . .
. . . .
. . . .
. . . .
. . . .
. . . .
. . . .
. . . .

24 MAY

Opening up to the energy around us can be very calming indeed. Find a calm spot and sit with your eyes closed. Concentrate on how your skin feels. Is there a light breeze? A sense of warmth? Does the energy around you feel buzzing and frenetic or calm and still?

. . . .
. . . .
. . . .
. . . .
. . . .
. . . .
. . . .
. . . .
. . . .

25 MAY

One summer, the kids and I painted an underwater mural on our garden wall. It's certainly no Monet, but it's a real family masterpiece. Colours, paint splats and darting fish all remind us of fun and adventure. Is there a space in your home for a little creativity? Can you create your own masterpiece that evokes happy and calming memories?

26 MAY

If you are edging towards the end of May feeling slightly overwhelmed and stressed can you try to take the edge off with some physical exercise or deep breathing? Bringing it back to the physical helps us to calm our nervous system and alleviate the mind.

27 MAY

Can you take time to
lie down today and run
a mental scan over your
body to see where any
tension lies? Are you tight
in the chest? Tense in the
shoulders? What feels
good and what areas need
more calm and attention?

28 MAY

Hopefully the weather is now warming up. Time to box away those thick black tights and crack open the flip-flops. Maybe it's even time for a winter clothes cull? I hear the charity shop calling!

....

....

....

....

....

....

....

....

....

....

....

....

....

....

....

....

....

....

29 MAY

Sometimes a change of scenery is a simple and good way of dissipating stress. Can you plan a little daytrip to a beautiful natural spot? The coast or perhaps a National Trust area?

. . . .
. . . .
. . . .
. . . .
. . . .
. . . .
. . . .
. . . .

. . . .

30 MAY

When you're having a clear-out at home, hold each object or piece of clothing in your hands and see if that item brings you joy. If not, or if you haven't worn it or used it for over a year, maybe it's time to let it go. Having a good clear-out is a brilliant way to refresh the energy in your home.

. . . .
. . . .
. . . .
. . . .
. . . .
. . . .
. . . .
. . . .

31 MAY

What moments or people brought you calm this month?

. . . .

. . . .

. . . .

. . . .

. . . .

. . . .

. . . .

. . . .

. . . .

. . . .

. . . .

. . . .

. . . .

. . . .

. . . .

. . . .

JUNE

Do you think you have found your own voice at this point in life? I'll be honest with you, I feel I'm JUST finding mine now. I may seem confident and the job I do would perhaps suggest I've always felt this way, but no, I'm just getting into the groove of feeling confident now. This doesn't mean that for the last 21 years my working life and the words I've spoken have been a lie or inauthentic; I just feel that now I can tell my story, let my opinions flow and chip into debates and discussions with a confidence I perhaps lacked before.

Make June the month to work on that inner confidence and flex those vocal muscles in the best way possible. If you're shy and retiring, known as a chatterbox, or sit somewhere in between, there is still always room to grow.

Once we have located how that voice sounds we can jump in on conversations with excitement and confidence, we can let go of the post-conversation paranoia and reduce the stress of others disagreeing with our own thoughts. This doesn't mean we have to be arrogant or indeed closed off to other opinions around us, it simply means we get to be 100 per cent authentic and completely ourselves when around others, which always brings the calm in heavy doses. Breathe confidence into that voice and speak the truth always.

1 JUNE

What words are you desperate
to say but feel you can't?
Do you long to tell someone
you love them? Do you have
pent-up rage because you
haven't voiced an injustice
you have felt? Rather than
blurt anything out or feel like
the thoughts are trapped, use
this space to write down the
locked-up words.

2 JUNE

Letter writing is a great way to construct some confidence. Through writing down your thoughts and feelings and addressing them to another or even yourself, we can admit certain emotions to ourselves. You don't even have to post it afterwards – simply writing them down helps to release the potency of the words you need to let go of.

3   JUNE

This page is all about speaking YOUR truth. What really makes you . . .

ANGRY?:

SORROWFUL?:

HAPPY?:

FEEL GUILTY?:

FEEL FULL OF LOVE?:

4   JUNE

What subjects do you
feel most passionate
about in life?

FIND YOUR FUN ♥

5   JUNE

If you could say one thing
to your mum right now,
what would it be?

· ·

· ·

· ·

· ·

· ·

· ·

· ·

· ·

· ·

6   JUNE

If you could say one thing
to your dad right now,
what would it be?

· ·

· ·

· ·

· ·

· ·

· ·

· ·

· ·

7 JUNE

When there is conflict
within both your family
life and home life do
you shrink away from
confrontation? Do you
shout too loudly and get
into knots? Or do you
end up as a mediator for
others?

. . . .

. . . .

. . . .

. . . .

. . . .

. . . .

. . . .

. . . .

. . . .

8 JUNE

Maybe you share a flat
with friends, have children,
or live at home with your
parents. Cohabiting can
be the source of a lot
of love but also needs a
lot of cooperation and
balance. Do you feel there
is balance in your home/
family life? If the answer
is 'no', can you calmly
confront this situation?

. . . .

. . . .

. . . .

. . . .

. . . .

. . . .

. . . .

. . . .

. . . .

9   JUNE

Before you speak aloud
when in a group outside
your house, take a minute
to say a short mantra in
your head. Repeat the
mantra three times and
believe the power of the
words. Perhaps 'I am
confident, my words are
valued, my words matter'.
What would you like your
mantra to be?

10   JUNE

Do you use your voice at
work/university/school/
home? Do you feel your
words carry weight and are
truly what you want and
need to say?

11 JUNE

If you feel you could be more authentic, honest and confident when speaking outside the home, remember that lots of people struggle with this too. Even the most confident people out there will have huge moments of self-doubt around what they say out loud.

....
....
....
....
....
....
....
....
....

12 JUNE

Do you feel your voice and opinions are appreciated and respected in your home/family life?

....
....
....
....
....
....
....
....
....

13 JUNE

What words have you
been too scared to say?
And to who? Write them
a letter here. You needn't
post it, just see how it
feels to write the words
down.

· ·

· ·

· ·

· ·

· ·

· ·

· ·

· ·

· ·

· ·

· ·

· ·

· ·

· ·

· ·

· ·

· ·

14 JUNE

What do you wish you
HADN'T said? An
impulsive rant or angry
confrontation that causes
you stress to recall?

15 JUNE

What one word sums you up?

....
....
....
....
....
....
....
....
....

16 JUNE

A lack of confidence can actually make my voice sound different. Sometimes, on the way to work, I'll sing loudly just to wake my voice up so it sounds bold and open when I next speak.

....
....
....
....
....
....
....
....

17 JUNE

I know swearing is naughty but sometimes I do mutter or even shout certain swear words to release some tension. What's your favourite bad word?

....
....
....
....
....
....
....
....
....

18 JUNE

Has there ever been a moment where you have felt silly after saying something? God, I feel like this all of the time. I replay cringey moments on a loop in my head for weeks afterwards and wish I had put more thought into what I wanted to say. You are never alone with this toe-curler, believe me!

....
....
....
....
....
....
....
....

" CONFIDENCE ISN'T WALKING INTO A ROOM THINKING YOU'RE BETTER THAN EVERYONE, IT'S WALKING IN AND NOT HAVING TO COMPARE YOURSELF TO ANYONE AT ALL. "

19 JUNE

Do you owe someone an apology? Not always easy. Actually probably never easy but so relieving for all! Before you go for it, use this page to write down exactly what you want to say.

· ·

· ·

· ·

· ·

· ·

· ·

· ·

· ·

· · · · · · · · · · · · · · · · ·

20 JUNE

Do you find it difficult to say, 'I love you'? Can you trace back to why? Have you been very hurt previously? Are you scared of rejection?

· ·

· ·

· ·

· ·

· ·

· ·

· · · · · · · · · · · · · · · · · · · ·

· · · · · · · · · · · · · · · · ·

21 JUNE

Finding your voice isn't just about speaking. It's about knowing who you are, what makes you tick and what you believe in.

22 JUNE

I went to a spoken word session recently which was so terrifying but I got so much from it. I realised the true connection between feeling thoughts and emotions, writing them down and then freeing them by speaking them aloud.

23 JUNE

Being an introvert isn't about being quiet all of the time. Being an extrovert doesn't mean you're loud and brash. It's more about how being in a group of people affects your energy levels; whether you feel boosted or drained of energy after being around them.

24 JUNE

Do you find it hard to make decisions? I regularly stand at life's crossroads scratching my head, wishing someone else would point me in the right direction. When you get in to the swing of having your own voice and knowing what you're about, then decision making gets easier. Will your decision lead you one step closer to what truly makes you tick?

25 JUNE

How easily swayed are you by others' confidence? Sometimes I mistake others' words for the truth because of their vehement stance and opinion. Don't follow the crowd just because they are acting like they know it all.

26 JUNE

Remember it's okay to make mistakes. Knowing your own voice and feeling confident in your decisions doesn't make you invincible. It is so important that we all make mistakes along the way so we can learn and perhaps turn down new roads. Even when mistakes are made, feel calm in knowing it is A-okay.

27 JUNE

Teaming strong body language with your words is very important. What's the point of having a strong spice with loads of kick if the curry is all mushy and watery? There's a powerful and calming alchemy if you can match your words with confident body language.

28 JUNE

If you are feeling nervous to speak aloud, get your body ready for action even if your mind isn't 100 per cent onboard. Stand tall, push your chest out like a proud gorilla, and stand with your feet hip-distance apart. Own the space you're in and walk into a room with this air of confidence.

....
....
....
....
....
....
....
....
....

29 JUNE

What subjects in your life or community do you feel are worth speaking up for?

....
....
....
....
....
....
....
....
....

30 JUNE

What moments or people brought you calm this month?

....

....

....

....

....

....

....

....

....

....

....

....

....

....

....

....

JULY

July can be a month of extreme socialising, maybe only second to the big daddy of socialising: Christmas. Friends want to meet up for fun in the sun; to exchange stories about summer romances; or enjoy lazy, hazy afternoons on an itchy picnic rug with a crate of strawberries and Jazzy Jeff on Spotify (for the millennials or Gen Z reading this, swap Jazzy Jeff for Dua Lipa).

Does your own friendship circle fill you with calm and comfort or does it often lead to a little chaos? Do you have several friendship groups that offer up different levels of fun and frolic depending on the occasion? Does socialising in general make you want to run for the hills?

I feel very lucky that I have several very calm types in my life. I love being in their slow pace orbit, hearing their kind words and relaxing in to their content and cosy energy. This month is about celebrating those people in your life who are a constant calm. The mere mention of their name, or memory of their beaming face, relaxes those tense muscles around your neck and makes you exhale deeply. These friends are rare jewels to be treasured and thanked, so why not make July the month to honour these special souls and jump on their own personal bandwagon of calm.

1   JULY

What does calm mean
to you this month?

2 JULY

Who brings you the
most calm?

. . . .
. . . .
. . . .
. . . .
. . . .
. . . .
. . . .
. . . .

3 JULY

Who brings you the
most chaos?

. . . .
. . . .
. . . .
. . . .
. . . .
. . . .
. . . .
. . . .

4   JULY

My wedding anniversary!
*self-indulgent
moment* Memories of
complete calm and chaos.
So many beautiful people
dancing and laughing
and a constant calm that
everything was exactly
as it should be. Oh and
Happy Birthday, Dad, who
happens to be the calmest
person I know!

5   JULY

What social situations
make you feel very far
from calm?

6 JULY

What is your calmest
summer memory?

....
....
....
....
....
....
....
....
....

7 JULY

How do/does your best
friend/s make you feel calm?

....
....
....
....
....
....
....
....
....

8 JULY

At some point this week, get together your most treasured friends for a calm evening of good food and chatting about old times.

9 JULY

Have you ever been at a really busy party but had a moment of self-reflection and complete calm? A moment where the chaos writhes around you but you remain untouched by others' energies and feel still within yourself?

....
....
....
....
....
....
....
....................................
....

10 JULY

How does it make you feel when those around you gossip? You may feel fine with it but, like me, do you ever feel a little dirty afterwards? Be honest, no one is judging you.

....
....
....
....
....
....
....
....

11 JULY

Is there a member of your friendship group who you think needs a little calm influence? Can you be that person?

....

....

....

....

....

....

....

....

12 JULY

When others around you are floundering in chaos, how does it make you feel?

....

....

....

....

....

....

....

....

"

IT IS NOT YOUR JOB TO BE EVERYTHING TO EVERYONE.

"

13 JULY

When you walk into a room of people you don't know, how does it make you feel?

....
....
....
....
....
....
....
....
....

14 JULY

Next time you have to meet a group of new people and feel nervous about it repeat a small mantra in your head to help bring the calm to the surface. Perhaps 'I am calm, I am loved, I am supported'. Repeat this three times before you enter the room/venue.

....
....
....
....
....
....
....
....

15 JULY

Is there anyone in your life who seems addicted or drawn to chaos? Why do you think that is? Sometimes looking for the reasons and routing back can help us feel more empathetic and understanding of others.

16 JULY

What calming activity could you and your friends partake in this month? Socialising doesn't have to involve a bar or pub.

17 JULY

You're halfway through the month and indeed halfway through the year, so enjoy this breathing exercise below to help you take stock of what has been and prepare you for what is still to come.

Breathe in through your nose for four seconds, hold your breath for seven seconds, then exhale through your mouth for eight seconds. This helps us to come out of the mind, slow the heart rate and activate the parasympathetic nervous system to bring us into a relaxed state.

18 JULY

Having a 'staycation' can be a
lovely way to unwind and bring a
little calm into your world. Grab
a great mate and head off to be
a tourist in a part of the UK you
haven't been to before. I often
have tourist days in London
as there is always so much to
explore even after living here
my whole life. You don't have to
travel a great distance to get a
little break from the norm.

19   JULY

Enjoy those nights where you are alone. For me, it is important to have time like this to relax properly and conjure up some fresh energy. If it's warm, can you spend an evening outdoors reading a book or eating while simply admiring the evening sky?

. . . .
. . . .
. . . .
. . . .
. . . .
. . . .
. . . .
. . . .
. . . .

20   JULY

Be honest with people. I can sometimes get flustered if I have a social engagement to attend and know that I have an early start the next day, so I like to fess up to the host or friend that I will need to leave early. Otherwise I get nervous and stressed out trying to plot an escape route!

. . . .
. . . .
. . . .
. . . .
. . . .
. . . .
. . . .
. . . .

21 JULY

Why not go booze-free
for a week? So much of
today's socialising is based
around alcohol but I barely
drink these days. I don't
associate alcohol with
relaxing or calm as it rarely
brings me either of those.

22 JULY

Can you plan a social
engagement this coming
week that doesn't involve
alcohol at all. How does
that make you feel?

23 JULY

One of my friends
recently called me
'boring' for not drinking
with them. It is a strange
cultural myth that we
have created that alcohol
makes you or things more
fun. I would rather have
fun on my own terms and
without the hangover the
next day. That is my calm.

. . . .

. . . .

. . . .

. . . .

. . . .

. . . .

. . . .

. . . .

24 JULY

How many units of alcohol
do you think you've
consumed this month?

. . . .

. . . .

. . . .

. . . .

. . . .

. . . .

. . . .

. . . .

25 JULY

Who is your go-to
confidante? Do they make
you feel calm once you've
shared your fears and
concerns with them?

· ·

· ·

· ·

· ·

· ·

· ·

· ·

· ·

26 JULY

How do you feel after
you've shared a secret or
worry with a friend? Does
it bring you instant calm?

· ·

· ·

· ·

· ·

· ·

· ·

· ·

· ·

27 JULY

How would your friends
react if you didn't drink on
a night out?

. . . .

. . . .

. . . .

. . . .

. . . .

. . . .

. . . .

. . . .

. . . .

28 JULY

Always use calm friends to
bring you solace and peace
of mind, but make sure
you don't use them as a
dumping ground to offload
constantly! Take advice
and process it in a calm and
thoughtful way. Advice is
often a joyful gift.

. . . .

. . . .

. . . .

. . . .

. . . .

. . . .

. . . .

. . . .

29 JULY

Remember how important
it is to truly listen to a
friend. If they themselves
have a worry, if they
need advice, or if they
are offering you up some
much-needed wisdom –
don't just speak at them,
listen to what they have
to say.

30 JULY

Are you a calm
friend? How would
your closest friends
describe you?

31 JULY

What moments or people brought you calm this month?

....

....

....

....

....

....

....

....

....

....

....

....

....

....

....

....

AUGUST

Light evenings, sunshine (hopefully), holidays (maybe?), music festivals (yes please!), BBQs (pass the veggie sausages!), school's out, legs out, freckles out. We are now in peak summer mode and there's an awful lot going on. Does August fill you with calm warmth and breezy thoughts, or does it all feel a little frantic and overwhelming? I personally enjoy the summer months a lot as physically I feel like less of a scaly, old, dry-skinned dragon. I can feel the vitamin D soaking into my skin and bringing my cold bones back to life. Yet at times, I do feel the pressure to be making the most of every sunny moment. It can seem as if everyone you know is either on holiday somewhere sun-drenched and dreamy, or living it up in their local pub garden. Social media magnifies our knowledge of who is doing what and when. How many palm trees, hotdog legs on stripy towels, and sun-kissed noses will we all be witness to on social media this month? Bloody loads, that's how many!

Of course our regular lives can't cease to exist just because the evenings span out until 9pm and we still have the more mundane and monotonous chores, jobs and routines to carry out among it all. The summer doesn't have to be one long party if that's not how you roll and even those who look like they're living it up are probably only portraying a small fraction of their story. This month, let's banish FOMO, stop comparing ourselves and get the hell off our phones to welcome in the calm!

1 AUGUST

This month I hope to
find calm in . . .

....
....
....
....
....
....
....
....
....

2 AUGUST

I know I feel calm when
. . .

....
....
....
....
....
....
....
....

3 AUGUST

How many times have you looked on social media today? How did it make you feel?

....
....
....
....
....
....
....
....
....

4 AUGUST

Can you go a whole 24 hours without looking on any social media at all?

....
....
....
....
....
....
....
....
....

5   AUGUST

What assumptions have
you made about a friend
or person on social media
without really knowing the
true story?

. . . .

. . . .

. . . .

. . . .

. . . .

. . . .

. . . .

. . . .

6   AUGUST

What was the last image
you posted on social media?
Was it the whole story?

. . . .

. . . .

. . . .

. . . .

. . . .

. . . .

. . . .

. . . .

7 AUGUST

Do you ever get FOMO?
What are you really scared
of missing out on?

. . . .

. . . .

. . . .

. . . .

. . . .

. . . .

. . . .

. . . .

. . . .

. . . .

. . . .

. . . .

. . . .

. . . .

. . . .

. . . .

. . . .

8   AUGUST

Do you find yourself
comparing your life to
other people's online?
Remember we are all our
own worst enemy and
critic!

....

....

....

....

....

....

....

....

....

9   AUGUST

What are you proud of
this month? Can you
focus on these positives
to stop you from focusing
on everyone else's
achievements or highs?

....

....

....

....

....

....

....

....

10 AUGUST

Post a photo of yourself on Instagram that you feel is truly authentic to how you feel now. Whatever emotion you're feeling, however you're looking, and without filters or distortion. Simply YOU!

11 AUGUST

I find it so hard to leave my work to one side at times. I'm lucky I enjoy my job and I'm deeply ambitious in where I want to take it, so I get wrapped up in answering emails and researching subjects. I never give myself enough time to just BE! Shut the laptop and reconnect with being you.

12 AUGUST

Is there truly something you believe you're NOT doing that you wish you were? If so, rather than feeling envious of others, can you make that change in your own life? Also think about it; do you even really want that change?

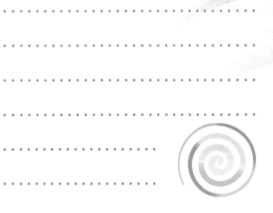

13 AUGUST

Don't be jealous, be inspired!

14 AUGUST

If you're feeling het up and can't focus on your own contentment today, draw some calm circles in this space or simply doodle to bring the focus back to the now and to the physical.

15 AUGUST

You're halfway through the month. Try this breathing exercise below to bring you back to the NOW and HERE.

....

....

....

....

....

....

....

....

Close your eyes. Place your thumb over your right nostril and exhale through the left nostril for eight counts. Breathe in through the left nostril and hold for another eight. Now repeat on the other side. Keep going up to 10 times and notice the difference in your breath.

16 AUGUST

Can you digitally detox today? If not fully then can you reduce your screen time?

. . . .
. . . .
. . . .
. . . .
. . . .
. . . .
. . . .
. . . .
. . . .

17 AUGUST

If you're finding it hard to leave social media alone today, why not use it to spread some joy? Post a photo of those you love and are thankful for. Show your gratitude and thanks to others.

. . . .
. . . .
. . . .
. . . .
. . . .
. . . .
. . . .
. . . .

18 AUGUST

Loads of my mates on social media seem to be . . . .
. . . . yet I'm not. And THAT'S OKAY!

. . . .

. . . .

. . . .

. . . .

. . . .

. . . .

19 AUGUST

Be completely honest
with yourself: do you
ever compare yourself
physically to those you see
on social media?

. . . .

. . . .

. . . .

. . . .

. . . .

. . . .

. . . .

. . . .

20 AUGUST

Honour and respect your own body and what it can do. If you don't look like those you see online, remember it's all an illusion anyway. Social media offers up small snippets of reality and certainly has no correlation to the calm and happiness of that individual. Feel proud of your own uniqueness and what you're capable of and let that confidence shine.

21 AUGUST

BE YOU! Write down here all you wish to celebrate about yourself today.

22 AUGUST

Don't worry about what you're NOT doing, enjoy what you ARE doing.

. . . .
. . . .
. . . .
. . . .
. . . .
. . . .
. . . .
. . . .
. . . .

23 AUGUST

Notice how often you reach for social media when you're feeling fidgety or edgy. Is it your 'go to' when you want to push feelings away?

. . . .
. . . .
. . . .
. . . .
. . . .
. . . .
. . . .
. . . .

24 AUGUST

Rather than checking in on what your friends are up to online, make an effort to get some proper face time in with them. Meet up and have a good natter in person. It's always way more fun and deeper-rooted all round: a much calmer way to communicate.

25 AUGUST

Feel calm knowing that your path won't look like anyone else's.

" PEOPLE WHO REPEATEDLY ATTACK YOUR CONFIDENCE AND SELF-ESTEEM ARE QUITE AWARE OF YOUR POTENTIAL, EVEN IF YOU ARE NOT. "

26 AUGUST

Do you spy on someone online? Do you find yourself skimming through an ex-boyfriend's Instagram page? Your old partner's new partner's Facebook profile? This is a form of self-torture! Try to implement some discipline around this kind of voyeurism and see how much better you feel.

27 AUGUST

A wise friend once said to me to be careful of what energy we let in to our lives and what energy we let out. When we are online we are letting in so much energy from others. Be choosy about this.

28 AUGUST

Do you feel calmer after being more vigilant about your own online habits this month?

....

....

....

....

....

....

....

....

29 AUGUST

How much of your self-worth comes from your online life? Don't let the balance tip. Your real life and the real you have so much to offer.

....

....

....

....

....

....

....

....

30 AUGUST

What did you feel calm
about today?

....

....

....

....

....

....

....

....

....

....

....

....

....

....

....

....

....

....

31 AUGUST

What moments or people brought you calm this month?

. . . .

. . . .

. . . .

. . . .

. . . .

. . . .

. . . .

. . . .

. . . .

. . . .

. . . .

. . . .

. . . .

. . . .

. . . .

SEPTEMBER

This month often feels like another chance to start again. It's the New Year without the pressure and hangover. It's back to school, bye bye lazy summer days and perhaps a time for change.

When I was at school I was proficient enough in the areas I enjoyed but I didn't view learning as a luxury. These days it is my favourite pastime. I truly understand the richness and splendour that it holds and with that comes calm.

The process of learning something new can be extremely calming as you set out on a new adventure, owning up to the fact that you're a beginner. There are no expectations, just a very open mind and willingness for exploration. Each time new information is devoured and stored, our worlds widen and open up. I wish I had fully grasped this concept when I was younger, but I was a dreamer and had other ideas. No regrets, as I wouldn't be in the position I am today if I hadn't been that way, and also perhaps wouldn't have such a thirst for learning as I do now!

Make September a month to learn more about yourself and others, and to give yourself a little reset to let the calm flood in.

1 SEPTEMBER

This month I hope to find calm in . . .

....
....
....
....
....
....
....
....

2 SEPTEMBER

This month's calm activity is . . .

....
....
....
....
....
....
....
....

3 SEPTEMBER

My birthday. An opportunity for me to lean in to and learn from a whole new year. What have you learned about yourself since your last birthday?

....
....
....
....
....
....
....
....
....

4 SEPTEMBER

What was your favourite subject at school and why?

....
....
....
....
....
....
....
....
....

5   SEPTEMBER

What do you know now
that you wish you had
known ten years ago?

· ·
· ·
· ·
· ·
· ·
· ·
· ·
· · · · · · · · · · · · · · · · ·
· · · · · · · · · · · · · · · · ·

6   SEPTEMBER

Is there anything you wish
you knew more about
now?

· ·
· ·
· ·
· ·
· ·
· ·
· · · · · · · · · · · · · · · · ·
· · · · · · · · · · · · · · · · ·

7 SEPTEMBER

Do you feel you have
the capacity to learn new
things at this point in life?
If not, then why?

....

....

....

....

....

....

....

....

....

....

....

....

....

....

....

....

....

....

8 SEPTEMBER

What would you love to
learn this month? Is there
a certain subject or skill
you would love to know
more about?

. . . .

. . . .

. . . .

. . . .

. . . .

. . . .

. . . .

. . . .

9 SEPTEMBER

Is there a friend who
would like to come on a
learning journey with you?
Maybe a local life drawing
class? A new fitness
session? An online course
to explore together?

. . . .

. . . .

. . . .

. . . .

. . . .

. . . .

. . . .

. . . .

10 SEPTEMBER

What has been your
greatest life lesson?
These moments in life
aren't always fun or
even pleasant, but it's
important to notice them
and understand what grew
from these times.

. . . .

. . . .

. . . .

. . . .

. . . .

. . . .

. . . .

. . . .

. . . .

11 SEPTEMBER

Can you recognise how
much learning comes from
tough experiences even
when they feel hellish at
the time?

. . . .

. . . .

. . . .

. . . .

. . . .

. . . .

. . . .

. . . .

. . . .

12 SEPTEMBER

Think back to when you last learned something. What was it and how did it feel?

13 SEPTEMBER

Be calm in the knowledge that it is never too late to learn. Even the wisest and most schooled and well-read souls have something to learn.

14 SEPTEMBER

Use this space to write your younger self a letter. Tell your younger self about all the brilliant things you've learned about YOU and life. Some of these lessons learned may have come out of very tough moments, but focusing on the positive 'lesson-learning' side of things helps ease the stress of tricky or painful memories.

15 SEPTEMBER

If I feel out of my depth and unsure about something someone else is talking about, I can feel quite panicky. In these moments, I would rather fess up and admit I don't understand than feel stuck in alienation and shame. Do you do the same or is this something you're willing to try? It always helps me navigate the stress of feeling inadequate.

16 SEPTEMBER

Remember, learning isn't purely about being academic. Learning is the willingness to see the world from different angles.

"THE EXPERT WAS ONCE A BEGINNER."

17 SEPTEMBER

I don't like walking into new situations feeling under-prepared. If I have a new job or work situation to tackle I always do as much research as I can beforehand so I can walk in to that space feeling calm. Don't wing it, research it!

. . . .
. . . .
. . . .
. . . .
. . . .
. . . .
. . . .
. . . .
. . . .

18 SEPTEMBER

Did you have a great teacher at school who imparted some wise advice or taught you a great life lesson?

. . . .
. . . .
. . . .
. . . .
. . . .
. . . .
. . . .
. . . .
. . . .

19 SEPTEMBER

Sometimes our greatest teachers in life are the people who trouble us the most. Those that cause tension, pain or friction. They bring out something in us that we want to ignore. They extract a part of our own story or personality that might need attention or help us to learn valuable life lessons.

20 SEPTEMBER

Who do you think is or has been your greatest teacher? This can be hard to admit when it is someone we feel we dislike or find tricky.

21 SEPTEMBER

Can you think of a
situation in your life that
is causing you stress? Is
there any way of seeing it
from another angle? It may
seem impossible at first but
are there other avenues to
walk down which may offer
up some calm?

. . . .

. . . .

. . . .

. . . .

. . . .

. . . .

. . . .

. . . .

. . . .

. . . .

. . . .

. . . .

. . . .

. . . .

. . . .

. . . .

. . . .

22 SEPTEMBER

If you are living through a sad, stressful or uncomfortable time, hold on to the thought that these can often be the birthplace of greatness and new-found strength.

. . . .
. . . .
. . . .
. . . .
. . . .
. . . .
. . . .
. . . .

23 SEPTEMBER

Learning requires a level of dedication but also a great portion of openness. Remaining flexible to newness gives us the room and scope to enter into new conversations and take on new information.

. . . .
. . . .
. . . .
. . . .
. . . .
. . . .
. . . .
. . . .

24 SEPTEMBER

Think back over the last
few weeks of this month.
What have you learned
about yourself and how
you react in stressful
situations?

. . . .
. . . .
. . . .
. . . .
. . . .
. . . .
. . . .
. . . .
. . . .

25 SEPTEMBER

Learning something new
often means we must
reject old patterns of
behaviour and old beliefs
and replace them with
new ones. I think that
personal expansion is
incredibly exciting but also
very calming. How does it
make you feel?

. . . .
. . . .
. . . .
. . . .
. . . .
. . . .
. . . .
. . . .

26   SEPTEMBER

Do you feel like this
month has acted as
somewhat of a fresh start?
How does that feel?

. . . .
. . . .
. . . .
. . . .
. . . .
. . . .
. . . .
. . . .
. . . .

27   SEPTEMBER

Is there a change in your
life you feel needs to be
made so you can have
a calmer existence? Sit
with your eyes closed and
picture in your mind the
change you want to see.
Imagine the images with
complete lucidity and
enjoy watching this change
occur in your mind.

. . . .
. . . .
. . . .
. . . .
. . . .
. . . .
. . . .
. . . .

28 SEPTEMBER

Remember to give yourself a break. If you are learning on the job, cramming for an exam, or have given yourself a lofty goal to reach, remember how important that breathing space is too. It is important to remind ourselves that the mind should take the back seat at times so the body can simply be.

29 SEPTEMBER

It's okay to NOT know.
In this day and age we
can feel such pressure to
know everything. What
everyone is doing all the
time. Where everyone
is all the time. What and
who are cool. It's A-okay
to not know everything all
of the time.

What moments or people brought you calm this month?

. . . .

. . . .

. . . .

. . . .

. . . .

. . . .

. . . .

. . . .

. . . .

. . . .

. . . .

. . . .

. . . .

. . . .

. . . .

OCTOBER

My main nemesis in life is not having the aptitude to 'let go'. It's my Achilles heel, my weak spot, the very obvious solution that I try and ignore. I think this time of year, as we watch the leaves turn golden amber and fall to the ground, offers up a brilliant opportunity to practise this tried and tested way of alleviating stress; we welcome a new season and bid the previous one farewell. We have no choice but to let go and enjoy the change.

Due to my lack of willingness in this department, I have metaphorical bingo wings that need firming up! I need to exercise this part of my emotional wellbeing and apply it to life when things feel stressful.

Although perhaps that's exactly where I am going wrong; I'm trying too hard rather than simply letting what must be, be. What I'm trying to articulate is that I'm a control freak and that has very little use most of the time. Although we may view it as a form of strength at times or even power, really it is just fear masquerading as order.

So let October be the month where we really try to free ourselves of enforced control, and have a little more faith and hope and fluidity.

October, I'm ready to let go and welcome in the calm!

1 OCTOBER

I'm ready for some calm
October, what ya got?

. . . .

. . . .

. . . .

. . . .

. . . .

. . . .

. . . .

. . . .

. . . .

2 OCTOBER

My calm activity this
month will be . . .

. . . .

. . . .

. . . .

. . . .

. . . .

. . . .

. . . .

. . . .

. . . .

3   OCTOBER

Remember how good it
felt to be free as a kid. No
inhibitions and very little
worry about order. Can
you channel a little of this
today?

. . . .

. . . .

. . . .

. . . .

. . . .

. . . .

. . . .

. . . .

4   OCTOBER

When you feel out of
control, what is your go-to
habit? One that calms you
or one that worsens the
stress?

. . . .

. . . .

. . . .

. . . .

. . . .

. . . .

. . . .

. . . .

5 OCTOBER

Next time you feel out of control, see if you can focus on the word 'trust' and start to feel the anxiety melt out of your muscles. Trust in what you're experiencing and know it'll bring something new to learn from.

6 OCTOBER

Would you say you're a control freak? While I hate to admit it, I know sometimes I try to micromanage my life. I soon realise that I'm missing out on quite a lot by being too focused and narrow-minded about how my day will unfold. Be open and LET GO!

7 OCTOBER

How are you feeling now
the evenings are getting
darker earlier? Are you
finding it hard to let go
of summer or are you
enjoying the calm and
cosy darker nights?

. . . .

. . . .

. . . .

. . . .

. . . .

. . . .

. . . .

. . . .

. . . .

8 OCTOBER

When we feel panic,
it's usually because
we are consciously or
subconsciously focusing
only on the future. Can you
shift your gaze back to right
now. How do you feel when
you eradicate any thought
of what lies ahead? Can
you let go of the worry and
welcome in some calm?

. . . .

. . . .

. . . .

. . . .

. . . .

. . . .

. . . .

9 OCTOBER

What big changes have you been through this year and how did they make you feel? Did you relax into them with ease or fight against the newness somewhat? Notice how you reacted to these moments in life and what your stress and calm levels around them were.

10 OCTOBER

If you have ever felt scared about change and have found it hard to let go of the old, can you route back to where that fear comes from?

11 OCTOBER

When I get stressed and lose sight of calm it's usually because I'm trying to go against what is naturally supposed to be occurring. I get too wrapped up in trying to keep control of a situation and forget to let go and trust. Do you do the same?

" SOMETIMES MEMORIES SNEAK OUT OF OUR EYES AND ROLL DOWN OUR CHEEKS. "

12 OCTOBER

When you feel stressed or like you are grappling with control, how do you feel physically? I'll often get mysterious headaches and neck ache. Not so mysterious when I think about it. Imagine all of that tension building physically – of course it needs an outlet somewhere. Another incentive to let go and allow calm in.

13 OCTOBER

Good moments must fade like a delicious perfume. Let their scent weaken naturally and fade to a more distant, yet equally as comforting, smell.

14 OCTOBER

As well as letting go of sad times, we must also let go of good times. Allow great moments and euphoric climaxes in life to naturally drift away in their own time. If we hold on too hard to the good times without honouring their ephemeral nature, then we risk becoming frustrated and ill at ease.

....
....
....
....
....
....
....
....
....

15 OCTOBER

Don't look backwards. You're not going that way.

....
....
....
....
....
....
....
....

"INHALE
THE
FUTURE,
EXHALE
THE
PAST.
"

16 OCTOBER

Try this simple exercise to help you let go of a past event. Imagine a symbol or picture that represents the event, sitting inside a large, robust-looking bubble. Picture it vividly and focus on how it makes you feel for a short time. Now place all of those emotions and feelings in the bubble with the symbol and watch it slowly float away up, up in to the sky. Keep imagining this bubble until it becomes a small dot on the horizon.

17 OCTOBER

Rather than zoning in on the lack of light in the evenings and the loss of the warmer days, can you focus on the cosiness of the colder weather and the beautiful colours of the autumn leaves?

18 OCTOBER

Loss is an incredibly difficult thing to get our human heads around. How can we ever feel okay about someone not being in our lives any more? There is no shortcut to healing, yet the passing of time and days helps incrementally to distance ourselves from that acute pain. It may never go, but it can change shape and texture over time.

19 OCTOBER

Most of us have a narrative in our heads about the people around us. 'So and so is awful because they do x, y and z.' We are all constantly labelling others and situations with a good or bad sticker. Letting go of these labels helps us change our personal perspective and allows calm in. Have you given those around you labels? If so who?

20 OCTOBER

Is it possible that any of the labels you have given others are heightened or exaggerated to make you feel safe? Do you vilify certain acquaintances or family members to feel you have the upper hand?

21 OCTOBER

Letting go of the labels
we place on people
can be tricky but it is
certainly freeing. If there
is someone in your life
you believe is tricky, write
their name down here and
then think about how your
version of them might not
be the full story.

22 OCTOBER

Letting go of habitual
behaviour you know no
longer serves you can be
incredibly calming. What
behavioural bad habits do
you know you want to get
rid of?

23 OCTOBER

Can you let go of labels
you've placed on yourself?
'I'm no good at speaking
in public as I get nervous.'
'I'm a useless cook.' 'I just
can't find love.' These are
labels we give ourselves
and then live by. We
short-change ourselves
and stop newness and
calm from flowing in.

24 OCTOBER

Letting go of fear can feel near
impossible, but there are small
steps that can be taken in the
right direction. If you were
scared of swimming as a small
child, perhaps you took baby
steps in to the shallow end
at first and then built up the
courage to walk a little further
out each time. Let go of fear
slowly rather than throwing
yourself in the deep end.

25 OCTOBER

How calm do you feel this
month?

. . . .

. . . .

. . . .

. . . .

. . . .

. . . .

. . . .

. . . .

. . . .

26 OCTOBER

Have you let go of
anything or anyone
recently? How did it feel?

. . . .

. . . .

. . . .

. . . .

. . . .

. . . .

. . . .

. . . .

27 OCTOBER

What is the difference between surrendering and giving up? I believe that giving up is through lack of trying and thought, and surrendering is an inner acknowledgement that a new path is needed.

28 OCTOBER

Are you able to let go of other people's words? I have been told certain things about myself over the years that I believe to be untrue. I've also been told things that possibly were true but were very hard to hear. Can you begin to let go of these words and their potency and stick to what you know deep down, or, if they are true, to accept them?

29 OCTOBER

Are there points of tension in your body that you would like to release? Lie on the floor and focus on that area and the stresses associated with it. Breathe fully into that area, focusing on loosening the tension and letting go of what emotionally is held there.

30 OCTOBER

Happy birthday to my husband, Jesse! Jesse gave up drinking alcohol quite a few years ago now which was a huge moment of change and letting go, so I dedicate this day to his courage and sobriety. Who would you like to dedicate this entry to? Who has made a great change in your life?

31 OCTOBER

Happy Halloween! What moments or people brought you calm this month

. . . .

. . . .

. . . .

. . . .

. . . .

. . . .

. . . .

. . . .

. . . .

. . . .

. . . .

. . . .

. . . .

. . . .

. . . .

NOVEMBER

Hands up who is shit at resting. 'ME ME ME!' *hands waving in the air like an attention-seeking child*. I'm the WORST at giving myself down-time and a break. Partly because I feel I have so much to do that days seem to whizz by and years seem to condense over time. I want to create, live, laugh, learn, and there never seems to be enough time.

Yet I'd be lying to myself, and you, if I didn't admit that I'm also a little scared to stop. What would happen if I just lounged around and relaxed? I have created weird rules that trap me into thinking that if I don't keep up the pace and stay on top of it all, it'll all fall apart. My career will cease to exist; the mountain of washing will rise so high that it will take over the downstairs floor of our house; and that I'll count for nothing. That last admission is probably the crux of it. I believe I sort of, well, won't exist. If I'm not 'doing' then who am I? This is where that handy old phrase 'we are human BEINGS not DOINGS', really needs to infiltrate my brain and set up camp.

This one for me is a work in progress. I love being active, busy and creative so part of me doesn't want to stop because of the adrenaline-fuelled kick I get from it all, but I know that if I do not rest then I can't actually do all the things I so desperately want to do. Rest is important and fundamental in the world of calm. We must rejuvenate, recuperate and have a little dose of nothingness to give us the impetus to BE and DO in whichever manner we so desire. I have a feeling I will be scribbling like mad in the following pages. Let November be the month of rest and plenty of calm.

1   NOVEMBER

This month I hope to find
calm in . . .

. . . .

. . . .

. . . .

. . . .

. . . .

. . . .

. . . .

. . . .

. . . .

2   NOVEMBER

Are you any good at
resting and relaxing?
Or are you a fidget-
pants like me?

. . . .

. . . .

. . . .

. . . .

. . . .

. . . .

. . . .

. . . .

3 NOVEMBER

How are your energy levels this month? Are you feeling the benefits of rest or are you running on empty?

....
....
....
....
....
....
....
....
....

4 NOVEMBER

Is there any room or slack for you to have a little more rest? If you have a full-on job or have a family it can seem nearly impossible. This is where we must ask for help.

....
....
....
....
....
....
....
....
....

5 NOVEMBER

Firework night isn't always the most peaceful night if you have scared pets or children that are awoken by booming rockets and whizzing Catherine wheels. Try not to build up too much anxiety around this and know that tomorrow normality will hopefully resume and you'll all catch up on a little rest. Or if you love firework night, get yourself out there and have some fun!

6 NOVEMBER

Is there anyone that can help lighten your load? Do you have a friend who can help you with anything? A family member who you can delegate some of the personal chaos to?

7 NOVEMBER

Write down the percentage of time you think each of the below takes up in your daily life:

FAMILY . . . . %   **SOCIALISING** . . . . %
FRIENDS . . . . %   **HOUSEWORK** . . . . %
WORK . . . . %   **REST** . . . . %

. . . .

. . . .

. . . .

8 NOVEMBER

Do you feel you need more rest?

. . . .

. . . .

. . . .

. . . .

. . . .

. . . .

. . . .

. . . .

9 NOVEMBER

Have you ever tried an online yoga nidra mediation? There are hundreds on YouTube. Find one, pop in some headphones and take an hour out of your day or evening to listen and relax. It's quite magical on many levels.

. . . .
. . . .
. . . .
. . . .
. . . .
. . . .
. . . .
. . . .
. . . .

10 NOVEMBER

Relaxing doesn't have to mean sleeping, expensive spa days or even being static. I find I feel super-rejuvenated after a long walk in the park. Walk in silence with your phone safely popped in your pocket and just breathe in the sights and smells around you.

. . . .
. . . .
. . . .
. . . .
. . . .
. . . .
. . . .
. . . .

11 NOVEMBER

If you feel there is no time in your day for YOU or some relaxation, can you build it in to your schedule? Can you walk to work or college instead of getting the bus or sitting in rush-hour traffic?

....

....

....

....

....

....

....

....

12 NOVEMBER

I have young kids who wake VERY early most days. This always leaves me slightly frazzled. I try to get to bed nice and early each night, to not drink too much alcohol and to eat well to counterbalance the impact it has on my body. Do you feel you get enough sleep? How do you help yourself when you don't?

....

....

....

....

....

....

....

....

"YOUR SPEED DOESN'T MATTER, FORWARD IS FORWARD."

13 NOVEMBER

I occasionally get insomnia which
is horrendous. I have learned some
visualisations over the years which can
help. One is to picture the first colour
that pops into your head. Breathe it
in through your nose then imagine
breathing the same colour out again.
Allow another random colour to pop
into your head and repeat. This takes
the focus off the annoyance and anxiety
around not sleeping and allows you to
slowly bring down your heart rate too.

14 NOVEMBER

What is your favourite way
to relax?

15 NOVEMBER

I love to draw and scribble with a biro. I find it deeply relaxing. Use this entry to let your pen or pencil run wild. Doodle or draw freely here.

16 NOVEMBER

How many hours a day are you spending on a screen? Do you think you could reduce this time down?

17 NOVEMBER

Can you start to give yourself a cut-off time when you put your phone away each night? I put my phone on aeroplane mode by 9pm so I'm not tempted to get lost on social media and get too stimulated by the light emanating from the screen. Less screen time equals more rest for our weary brains and certainly more calm.

....

....

....

....

....

....

....

....

....

18 NOVEMBER

What bad habits do you have that stop you from letting in calm and relaxing?

....

....

....

....

....

....

....

....

....

19 NOVEMBER

Have you relaxed much
this month so far?

. . . .

. . . .

. . . .

. . . .

. . . .

. . . .

. . . .

. . . .

20 NOVEMBER

How do you feel when
there is no stimulation
around? No screens, no
phone, no magazines or
papers, and no one to talk
to? Does it make you feel
a little edgy? Can you
learn to enjoy the calm
that lies in nothingness?

. . . .

. . . .

. . . .

. . . .

. . . .

. . . .

. . . .

21 NOVEMBER

Are you a people pleaser? Do you say yes to social events as you don't want to let people down or miss out? It is more than okay to say no sometimes and to have an evening in to just relax and be content in your own company.

22 NOVEMBER

Tonight, cook a comforting
meal that you know will
be enjoyable to prepare
and restorative to eat.
Something wholesome and
nutritious. What would you
like that to be?

23 NOVEMBER

Resting isn't being lazy or
slobbing about. Resting
is about giving yourself
time to physically and
emotionally recover,
reflect and recuperate.

24 NOVEMBER

Animals hibernate for the winter and I often feel personally inclined to do that too. I love to hunker down at home in cosy clothes and warm blankets and eat comforting food with the lights low. I adore the feeling of winter cosiness. Fancy getting cosy tonight?

. . . .
. . . .
. . . .
. . . .
. . . .
. . . .
. . . .
. . . .
. . . .

25 NOVEMBER

Self-care can be an incredibly cringey term to use and can feel a tad luxurious and frivolous to incorporate into our own lives. Yet it is of paramount importance to us all. If we are unhealthy, feel mentally imbalanced or over-tired, we cannot be of any help to others.

. . . .
. . . .
. . . .
. . . .
. . . .
. . . .
. . . .
. . . .

26 NOVEMBER

If you generally give yourself a hard time and don't let yourself rest, then make TODAY the day to apply a little self-care. Have a long bath, eat beautiful food and be kind to yourself.

. . . .
. . . .
. . . .
. . . .
. . . .
. . . .
. . . .
. . . .
. . . .

27 NOVEMBER

If you have a habit of being tough on yourself think of what you might say to a friend if they came to you complaining they were over-tired. You would probably tell them to rest up and take a step back. Try to apply the same advice to your own life.

. . . .
. . . .
. . . .
. . . .
. . . .
. . . .
. . . .
. . . .

28 NOVEMBER

How many hours sleep did you get last night? Can you aim for at least 8 tonight?

....
....
....
....
....
....
....
....
....

29 NOVEMBER

How did you sleep last night?

....
....
....
....
....
....
....
....
....

30 NOVEMBER

What moments or people
brought you calm this month?

....

....

....

....

....

....

....

....

....

....

....

....

....

....

....

....

....

....

....

....

NOVEMBER

DECEMBER

Is this perhaps the month where calm eludes us the most? The whole month seems to be drenched in tinsel-covered mayhem.

It's perhaps no surprise that by the time the twelfth month of the year has arrived we are relatively frazzled – yet we are expected to do so much. Buy Christmas presents for the masses, socialise like an 'it girl' and spend vast amounts of time with family members we might not normally choose to. It's FULL ON. During this month I turn into a list-writing machine, categorising gift lists for workmates, friends and family; lists for food shopping for certain family events and cook-ups; and lists to remind me not to forget about all the lists. I slightly lose the plot all round. I say yes to too many Christmas parties and then end up wanting to back out when the time arrives and always forget at least one Christmas present that I was supposed to buy. Mayhem.

The caveat to the chaos is that I usually thoroughly enjoy most of it and especially love watching my children's faces sparkle with delight when we approach Christmas Eve. They have brought such joy and twinkle to Christmas and for that I'm very grateful.

For some of us, this month can feel explosive as there is an expectation for jubilation with little regard to what has been before. If you have experienced a rough time around Christmas, even the faintest whiff of a mince pie can be evocative enough to make us wanna run a mile. December has its own scent, flavour, sound and feel so if it's rem-iniscent of a tough time, it seems even more potent. This month needs to be about either accepting the chaos or trying to reduce it somewhat. Can you find the calm in the chaos? Let's give it a bloody good go!

1 DECEMBER

This month I would like to
find the calm in . . .

....

....

....

....

....

....

....

....

2 DECEMBER

My calm activity this
month will be . . .

....

....

....

....

....

....

....

....

3 DECEMBER

Here's a chance to write
out any lists you know
need to hit the paper to
make you feel that bit
calmer. Is it a gift list?
A food shopping list or
simply thoughts that you
need out of your head?

....

....

....

....

....

....

....

....

....

4 DECEMBER

What feels chaotic to you
about this month?

....

....

....

....

....

....

....

....

5 DECEMBER

Are you the sort that enjoys a little chaos? How do you react to it?

....
....
....
....
....
....
....
....
....

6 DECEMBER

What is stressing you out at the moment?

....
....
....
....
....
....
....
....

7 DECEMBER

Can you delegate to those around you to get more help? Sometimes it feels very tricky to ask for help but usually there'll be a friend who is more than happy to give their time to you. Friends are bloody lovely, right?!

8 DECEMBER

Create some calm around the chaos of December. Can you create a calm atmosphere at home tonight? Some candles, a good book or chilled company?

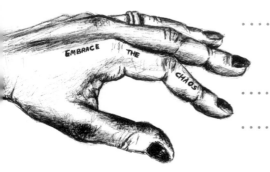

9 DECEMBER

It's not always the chaos that causes us stress but instead the way in which we react to it. Make a choice to take a moment and a good few deep breaths before sending back an angry text message, firing off an explosive email or shouting when confronted. Take back the control by remembering you have a choice. Does this feel possible?

10 DECEMBER

Do you combat the hectic nature of December by drinking? The office work party, reunions with old friends and family get-togethers? Have you tried socialising sober? How does it feel to you?

11 DECEMBER

December can make some feel very lonely. Do you know someone who needs a friend right now?

12 DECEMBER

Don't be a people pleaser.
If you need a night in
or time away from the
Christmas social scene, be
honest with those around
you and take time to rest.

....

....

....

....

....

....

....

....

13 DECEMBER

This can be a very
expensive month which
is never very calming.
Have you tried giving
your mates and family
homemade Christmas
gifts? Chutneys, caramel
dipping sauce, or biscotti
all make cheap and well-
thought-out gifts for
loved ones.

....

....

....

....

....

....

....

....

14 DECEMBER

As we near the big day write down here what you really want out of the festive period. Is it a fun-filled party-tastic whirlwind or is it actually a cosy and calm time?

15 DECEMBER

What triggers your stress?
Can you identify that
feeling creeping in and
what the catalyst is?

. . . .

. . . .

. . . .

. . . .

. . . .

. . . .

. . . .

. . . .

. . . .

16 DECEMBER

Remember you are not
stress. You are not chaos.
These are feelings that
come and then go again.

. . . .

. . . .

. . . .

. . . .

. . . .

. . . .

. . . .

. . . .

. . . .

17 DECEMBER

Being grateful for what we have each day allows us to focus on the calming positives. What are you grateful for today?

....
....
....
....
....
....
....
....
....
....
....
....
....
....
....
....
....
....
....

18 DECEMBER

If you are working over Christmas, why not have an early Christmas gathering this week to spend time with your loved ones? Make Christmas work for you and make it as big or small as feels comfortable.

. . . .

. . . .

. . . .

. . . .

. . . .

. . . .

. . . .

. . . .

. . . .

19 DECEMBER

I always find baking to be the most relaxing of hobbies and especially love it at Christmas time. Gingerbread men, spicy fruit loaves and suet-free mince pies are my go-to bakes. Why not try it yourself this week?

. . . .

. . . .

. . . .

. . . .

. . . .

. . . .

. . . .

. . . .

. . . .

20 DECEMBER

Smell can be very evocative and very calming. We have a Christmas spray at home that was loved by Jesse's late mother, Krissy. We spritz it all around the house to remind Jesse of his mum at this time of year. It's a gorgeous smell.

21 DECEMBER

If you and your partner or best mate are stumped as to what to buy for each other this Christmas, how about an experience you can both enjoy? Afternoon tea somewhere or a road trip to the calming coast?

22 DECEMBER

My kids tend to get very overexcited this month which fizzes the energy all around. I try not to get overwhelmed when this happens and keep reminding myself normality will resume shortly. How does the overexcitement of this time of year make you feel?

....

....

....

....

....

....

....

....

....

23 DECEMBER

Have you found any calm this month so far?

....

....

....

....

....

....

....

....

....

"

IF YOU'RE ALWAYS RACING TO THE NEXT MOMENT, WHAT HAPPENS TO THE ONE YOU'RE IN?

"

24 DECEMBER

I think I prefer Christmas
Eve to the big day itself.
There's a magic that fills
the air now I have kids and
I'm forever grateful for
that. What sort of magic
can you find in today?

25 DECEMBER

Call someone who might
be feeling lonely. Send
them a little calm and joy.
And Merry Christmas!

26 DECEMBER

Do you feel frazzled today or full of love (and potatoes)? Relax into whatever that feeling is.

27 DECEMBER

The few days between Christmas and New Year can feel very discombobulating – whether you're already back at work or still slobbing in your PJs. It's festive limbo-land. Is there a good festive film you can enjoy with others, or some fun and experimental cooking with leftover food you could try?

. . . .

. . . .

. . . .

. . . .

. . . .

. . . .

. . . .

. . . .

28 DECEMBER

I weirdly find this a good week to start to declutter my house and get rid of the old. I like to finish the year with a clear-out ahead of January. It fills me with calm. Could this work for you too?

. . . .

. . . .

. . . .

. . . .

. . . .

. . . .

. . . .

29 DECEMBER

If you feel a slight anticlimax after the excitement of Christmas, look to writing a list of hopes and positive ideas for the year ahead.

30 DECEMBER

Have a brisk walk in the great outdoors and get your body moving. I love to have lots of early morning winter runs at this time of year to wake me from the Christmas slumber.

31 DECEMBER

If, like me, you choose
to go to bed on New
Year's Eve at 9.30pm like
any other night, don't
worry about it or feel
embarrassed. I'm quite
proud of my granny-like
tendencies these days.
Go with what feels right
for you. What do you
have planned?

. . . .
. . . .
. . . .
. . . .
. . . .
. . . .
. . . .
. . . .

. . . .
. . . .
. . . .
. . . .
. . . .
. . . .
. . . .
. . . .
. . . .

THIS YEAR, WHO OR WHAT BROUGHT YOU CALM?

....

....

....

....

....

....

....

....

....

....

....

....

....

....

....

....

....

....

....

NOTES

....

....

....

....

....

....

....

....

....

....

....

....

....

....

....

NOTES

· ·

· ·

· ·

· ·

· ·

· ·

· ·

· ·

· ·

· ·

· ·

· ·

· ·

· ·

· ·

NOTES

NOTES

NOTES

....

....

....

....

....

....

....

....

....

....

....

....

....

....

....

NOTES